E

9046

D1196747

A Character Building Book™

Learning About the Work Ethic from the Life of
Cal Ripken, Jr.

Jeanne Strazzabosco

The Rosen Publishing Group's
PowerKids Press™
New York

Published in 1996 by The Rosen Publishing Group, Inc.
29 East 21st Street, New York, NY 10010

First Edition

Book design: Erin McKenna

Photo credits: Cover © Archive Photos; p. 8 © Brent Winebrenner/International Stock; p. 11 © Scott Thode/International Stock; all other photos © AP/Wide World Photos.

Strazzabosco, Jeanne.
    Learning about the work ethic from the life of Cal Ripken, Jr. / Jeanne Strazzabosco.
        p.   cm. — (A character building book)
    Includes index.
    Summary: A brief biography of the shortstop for the Baltimore Orioles, focusing on the hard work that he has put into his baseball career.
    ISBN 0-8239-2418-1
    1. Ripken, Cal, 1960– —Juvenile literature. 2. Baseball players—United States—Biography—Juvenile literature. 3. Baltimore Orioles (Baseball team)—Juvenile literature. [1. Work ethic—Juvenile literature. 2. Ripken, Cal, 1960–. 3. Baseball players. 4. Work ethics.] I. Title. II. Series.
GV865.R47S87 1996
796.357'092—dc20
[B]   96-21995
                                                                                 CIP
                                                                                  AC

Manufactured in the United States of America

Table of Contents

Like Father, Like Son

Cal Ripken, Jr., was born in 1960. He grew up in Aberdeen, Maryland. By the age of three, Cal knew that he wanted to be a baseball player when he grew up. He carried a ball and glove with him everywhere he went. His father, Cal, Sr., was a baseball player in the **minor leagues** (MY-ner LEEGZ) for the Baltimore **Orioles** (OR-ee-ulz). Cal traveled with his dad to practices and games around the country. His father taught him how to play baseball and to have a good **work ethic** (WERK EH-thik).

◄ *Cal's good work ethic helped him become the success that he is.*

Learning to Work Hard

Cal's parents raised him to expect a lot from himself. They taught him to be fair and honest, and that it takes hard work to meet your goals. Cal's goal was to become a **major league** (MAY-jer LEEG) ballplayer. He practiced for many, many hours. At his dad's games, Cal watched the players. He learned their plays and **strategies** (STRA-ta-jeez). At the end of each game, he always had questions for the players. He enjoyed being around his dad and the other ballplayers. He learned a lot from them.

Cal's parents taught Cal that it takes ▶
hard work to get what he wants.

Ballpark and Classroom

The ballpark was like a classroom for Cal. He wanted to do well, so he studied the way pitchers threw the ball. He watched how infielders **positioned** (poh-ZIH-shund) themselves. He saw how the ballplayers worked hard and played fair. His dad was a great teacher. He taught Cal to be a tough **competitor** (kom-PEH-tih-ter). In 1973, Cal showed how much he had learned. He helped his Little League team win the state championship. They went on to the national play-offs in Florida.

Cal discovered that a great way to learn how to play baseball well was by watching how the major league players played.

Try, Try Again

In his first year of high school, Cal tried out for the **varsity** (VAR-sih-tee) baseball team. Very few **freshmen** (FRESH-men) had ever made it onto a varsity team. At the tryouts, the coach said the boys had to run one mile in less than 6 minutes and 30 seconds. Cal tried his best. But he couldn't do it. He asked the coach if he could try again the next day. The coach was impressed that Cal was willing to try again. He agreed. The next day, Cal tried again. And this time he did it. He earned the right to be second baseman, then pitcher, on the team.

Ballplayers need to be able to run fast to make it from base to base like this player. Cal worked hard to be able to run fast enough. ▶

Always Learning

Cal didn't like to sit out when the other pitchers played. So he learned to play short-stop too. Cal's dad became one of the coaches of the Baltimore Orioles. Cal watched and learned from the major league players. He learned to throw a curve ball, a slider, and a change-up. He became much better than other high school ballplayers. When Cal wasn't playing baseball, he played soccer. He played well and was chosen as team captain. Cal worked hard in school too. He graduated from high school with an A average.

Cal learned new skills every chance he could.
◀ *He learned how to throw different kinds of pitches by watching major league games.*

Aiming High

During his senior year at Aberdeen High, talent scouts from many **professional** (pro-FEH-shun-ul) baseball teams came to watch Cal play. Several colleges were also interested in him. And the United States Military Academy wanted Cal to play on their soccer team. But Cal wanted to play professional baseball. In 1978, Cal was **drafted** (DRAF-tid) by the Baltimore Orioles.

All of Cal's hard work paid off when he was drafted by the Baltimore Orioles. ▶

The Major Leagues

Cal played for the Orioles' minor league teams. His dad had prepared him well. Cal was ready for the all-night bus rides and early morning practices. By 1981, Cal had made it to the Orioles' top minor league team, the Rochester Red Wings. He was named the International League's Rookie of the Year. Near the end of that season, he was called up to the Baltimore Orioles. It usually took players many years to make it to the major leagues. It had taken Cal only four years.

◀ *Cal made it to the major leagues faster than most ballplayers.*

Good Work Habits

Cal kept up his good work habits. He was a great player. His team members knew they could count on him to play well in every game. Cal was focused and kept on learning about the game. From the dugout, he watched players on other teams and learned from their mistakes. He started out as third baseman. The coach was so impressed with Cal that he moved him to shortstop, the hardest position to play. In 1982, Cal was voted Rookie of the Year. And in 1983, he received the American League's Most Valuable Player Award.

Cal's teammates and the Orioles' fans soon learned that they could always count on Cal to play hard and well. ▶

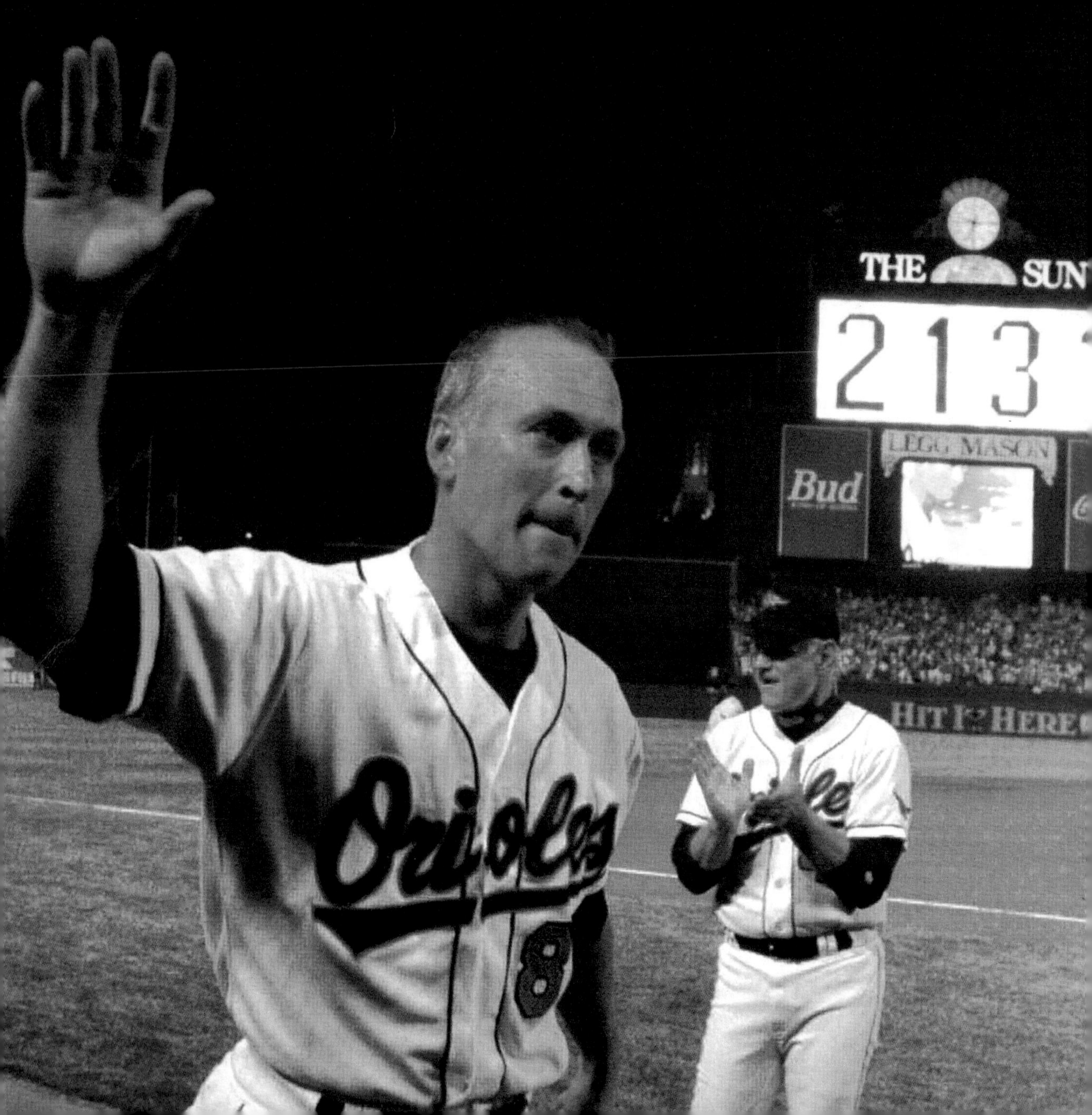
THE SUN
213
LEGG MASON
Bud
Orioles
8
HIT IT HERE

Breaking Records

In 1992, Cal signed a five-year **contract** (KON-trakt) with the Baltimore Orioles for $30.5 million. He received the American League's Outstanding Shortstop Award for two years in a row. One night in 1995, something even more amazing happened. Cal broke the **record** (REH-kerd) for playing the most major league baseball games in a row. The record was 2,130 games. That night Cal played his 2,131st **consecutive** (kon-SEK-yoo-tiv) game. It was a great moment for Cal and for baseball fans everywhere.

◄ *Cal's good work ethic led him to set a new record for playing the largest number of baseball games in a row. And the number is still growing.*

Giving It His Best

Cal has been very successful as a baseball player. Part of the reason is because he's naturally a good baseball player. But most of the reason is because he wants to do well and works very hard at his game. He thinks about and prepares for each game carefully. Cal has a great work ethic. He knows, and has shown the world, how far you can get if you work hard enough at something. Cal's nickname is Iron Man. He is a player who goes out on the field and gives it his best every day.

Glossary

competitor (kom-PEH-tih-ter) Person who competes with others.

consecutive (kon-SEK-yoo-tiv) In a row.

contract (KON-trakt) A written agreement.

drafted (DRAF-tid) To be asked to play a professional sport.

freshman (FRESH-man) First-year student.

major league (MAY-jer LEEG) Top-level professional baseball.

minor league (MY-ner LEEG) Lower-level professional baseball.

Orioles (OR-ee-ulz) One professional, major league baseball team.

position (poh-ZIH-shun) The way a person places himself.

professional (pro-FEH-shun-ul) Someone who is paid for what he does.

record (REH-kerd) The best yet done; best amount, rate, or speed yet reached.

strategy (STRA-ta-jee) Plan of action.

varsity (VAR-sih-tee) The top-level team representing a school.

work ethic (WERK EH-thik) Idea that work is important and that hard work is valuable.

Index